100 SOLOS
VIOLIN

Andante (Tchaikovsky) **71**
Arrivederci Roma **36**
As Long As He Needs Me **70**
(Theme from) A Summer Place **9**
The Ballad Of Davy Crockett **6**
Barcarolle (Offenbach) **72**
Be Back Soon **28**
Beautiful Dreamer **73**
Bibbidi-Bobbidi-Boo **21**
Blue Danube **74**
The Boatmen's Song Of The Volga **75**
Carnival Of Venice **76**
Celeste Aide **77**
Cielito Lindo **78**
Come Back To Sorrento **79**
Consider Yourself **48**
Dancing Queen **27**
Danny Boy (Londonderry Air) **41**
Drink To Me Only With Thine Eyes **87**
Days Of Wine And Roses **23**
The Drunken Sailor **20**
Edelweiss **3**
Emperor Waltz **80**
English Country Garden **13**
English Dance by J.C. Bach **57**
Fiddler On The Roof **49**
Food Glorious Food **19**
The Fool On The Hill **43**
The Happy Farmer **81**
Hasta Manana **64**
The Hawaiian Wedding Song **46**
He's Got The Whole World In His Hands **35**
How Can I Tell You **18**
Humoresque **82**
I'd Like To Teach The World To Sing **24**
I Don't Know How To Love Him **42**
Imagine **47**
Intermezzo **83**
Jealousy **65**
Knowing Me, Knowing You **61**
La Cucaracha **62**
La Paloma **84**
Lady **54**
Largo (from New World Symphony) **85**
Liebestraum **86**
Lillywhite **44**
Little Boxes **25**
Love Me Tender **8**
Love's Old Sweet Song **87**
Mexican Hat Dance **68**

Michelle **22**
Minuet by Boccherini **12**
Minuet by Mozart **11**
Minuet In G (Beethoven) **88**
Mockin' Bird Hill **32**
Mona Bone Jakon **16**
Morning Has Broken **4**
Narcissus **89**
Norwegian Wood **31**
Oh, What A Beautiful Mornin' **38**
Oon-Pah-Pah **14**
Penny Lane **55**
Pick A Pocket Or Two **6**
Popcorn **66**
Puff (The Magic Dragon) **17**
Return To Sender **45**
Reviewing The Situation **52**
Rivers Of Babylon **39**
Romeo And Juliet (Tschaikowsky) **60**
Saber Dance **90**
Sailing **10**
Scarborough Fair **8**
Sea Of Heartbreak **37**
Serenade (Schubert) **91**
Sgt. Pepper's Lonely Heart's Club Band **33**
She Loves You **53**
She's Leaving Home **15**
Smile **7**
Soldier's March (Schumann) **5**
Some Enchanted Evening **40**
Steptoe and Son **96**
Strawberry Fields Forever **51**
Strangers In The Night **29**
The Surrey With The Fringe On Top **58**
Thank You For The Music **63**
Theme from Concerto No. 1 (Tschaikovsky) **92**
Theme from Concerto No. 2 (Rachmaninoff) **93**
Turkey In The Straw **20**
Unfinished Symphony (Schubert) **94**
Waltz by Brahms **30**
When I'm Sixty-Four **43**
Where Have All The Flowers Gone? **7**
Where Is Love? **26**
Who Do You Think You're Kidding, Mr. Hitler? **69**
Who Will Buy? **56**
William Tell Overture **95**
With A Little Help From My Friends **50**
The Wonder Of You **13**
Wooden Heart **34**
You Never Done It Like That **59**

Music Sales America

DISTRIBUTED BY

HAL•LEONARD®
CORPORATION
7777 W. BLUEMOUND RD. P.O. BOX 13819 MILWAUKEE, WI 53213

This book Copyright © 1987 by Amsco Publications,
A Division of Music Sales Corporation, New York, NY.
All rights reserved.

Order No. AM 33671
International Standard Book Number: 978.0.8256.1095.0

Exclusive Distributors:
Music Sales Corporation
257 Park Avenue South, New York, NY 10010 USA
Music Sales Limited
8/9 Frith Street, London W1V 5TZ England
Music Sales Pty. Limited
120 Rothschild Street, Rosebery, Sydney, NSW 2018, Australia

Printed in the United States of America by
Vicks Lithograph and Printing Corporation

EDELWEISS (FROM "THE SOUND OF MUSIC").

Words by Oscar Hammerstein II. Music by Richard Rodgers.

MORNING HAS BROKEN.

Traditional.

SOLDIER'S MARCH.
by Schumann.

PICK A POCKET OR TWO.

Words and Music by Lionel Bart.

Moderato

THE BALLAD OF DAVY CROCKETT.

Word by Tom Blackburn. Music by George Bruns.

Moderato

WHERE HAVE ALL THE FLOWERS GONE.

Words and Music by Pete Seeger.

Moderato

SMILE.

Words by John Turner and Geoffrey Parsons. Music by Charles Chaplin.

Andante

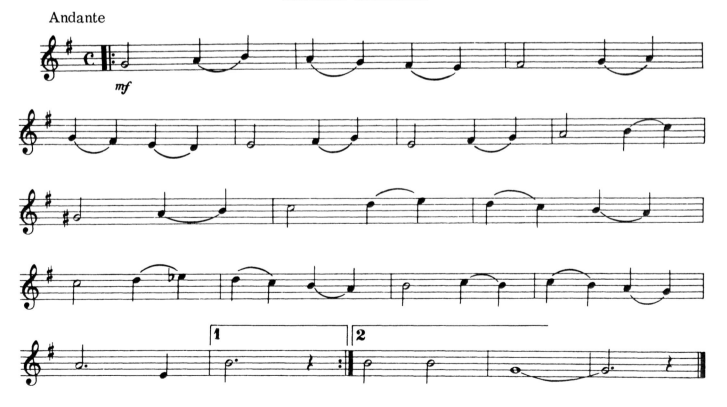

LOVE ME TENDER.

Words and Music by Elvis Presley and Vera Matson.

Moderately slow

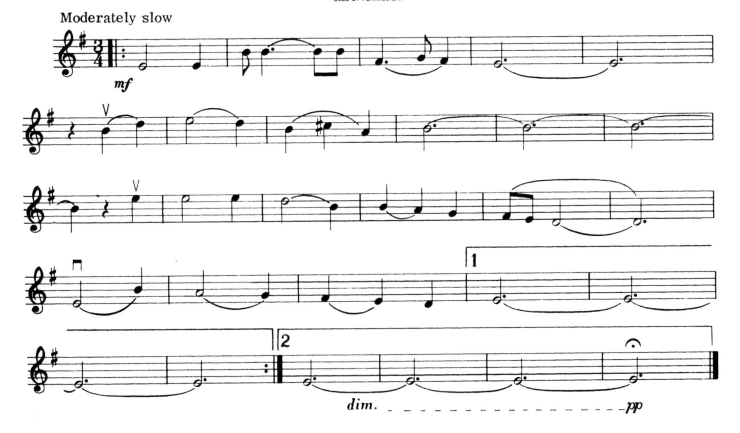

SCARBOROUGH FAIR.

Traditional.

Moderately slow

(THEME FROM) A SUMMER PLACE.

Music by Max Steiner.

SAILING.

Words and Music by Gavin Sutherland.

MINUET.

Mozart.

MINUET.

Boccherini.

THE WONDER OF YOU.

Words and Music by Baker Knight.

Slowly, with feeling

ENGLISH COUNTRY GARDEN.

Traditional.

Moderato

OOM-PAH-PAH (FROM THE COLUMBIA PICTURES-ROMULUS FILM "OLIVER").

Words and Music by Lionel Bart.

Brightly

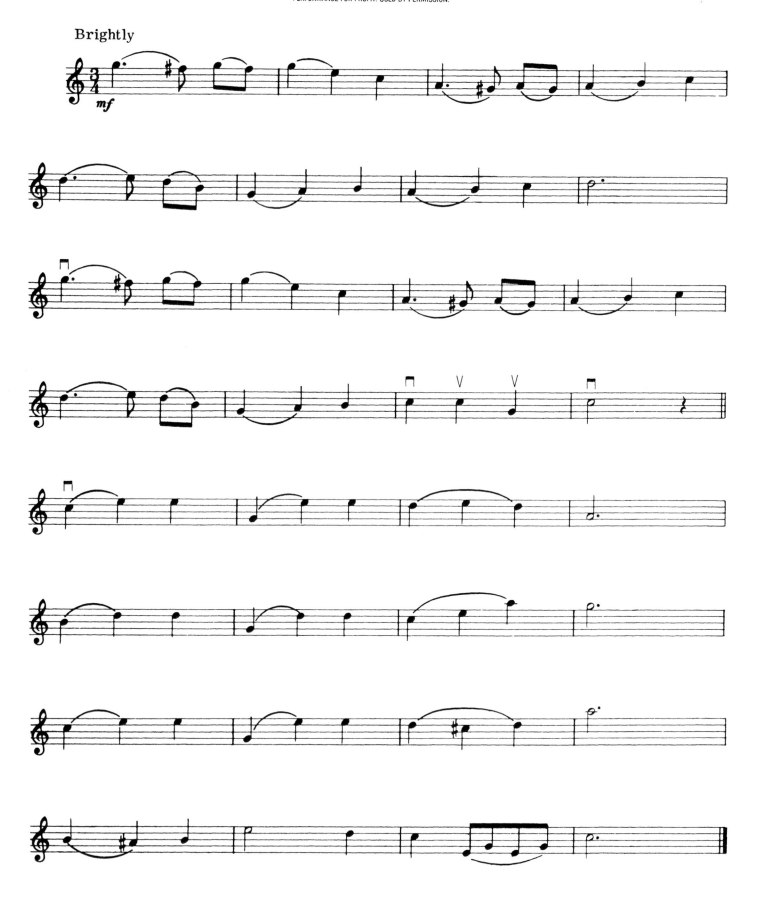

SHE'S LEAVING HOME.

Words and Music by John Lennon & Paul McCartney.

Moderato

MONA BONE JAKON.

Words and Music by Cat Stevens.

PUFF THE MAGIC DRAGON.

Words and Music by Peter Yarrow and Leonard Lipton.

HOW CAN I TELL YOU.
Words and Music by Cat Stevens.

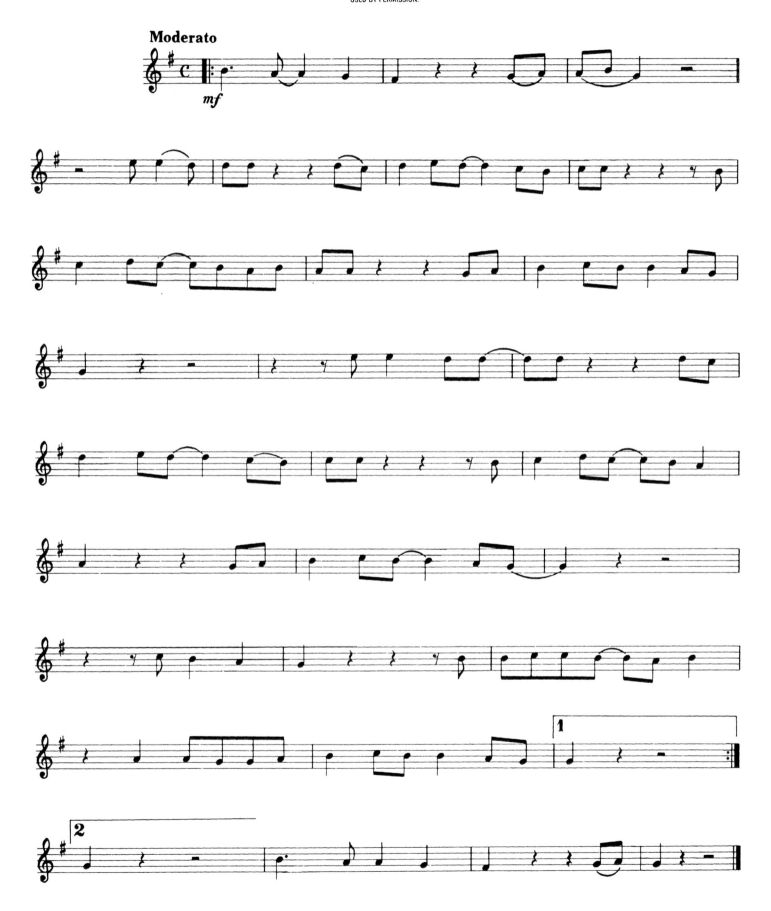

FOOD GLORIOUS FOOD (FROM THE COLUMBIA PICTURES-ROMULUS FILM "OLIVER").

Words and Music by Lionel Bart.

THE DRUNKEN SAILOR.

Traditional.

TURKEY IN THE STRAW.

Traditional.

BIBBIDI-BOBBIDI-BOO.

Words by Jerry Livingston. Music by Mack David and Al Hoffman.

Light Schottische tempo

MICHELLE.

Words and Music by John Lennon and Paul McCartney.

Moderato

DAYS OF WINE AND ROSES.

Words by Johnny Mercer. Music by Henry Mancini.

Moderato

I'D LIKE TO TEACH THE WORLD TO SING.

Words and Music by Roger Cook, Roger Greenaway, Billy Backer and Billy Davis.

Moderato

LITTLE BOXES.
Words and Music by Malvina Reynolds.

Moderate Waltz Tempo

WHERE IS LOVE (FROM THE COLUMBIA PICTURES-ROMULUS FILM "OLIVER").

Words and Music by Lionel Bart.

DANCING QUEEN.

Words and Music by Benny Andersson, Stig Anderson & Bjorn Ulvaeus.

BE BACK SOON (FROM THE COLUMBIA PICTURES-ROMULUS FILM "OLIVER").

Moderato

STRANGERS IN THE NIGHT.

Words by Charles Singleton and Eddie Snyder. Music by Bert Kaempfert.

Moderately slow

WALTZ.
by Brahms.

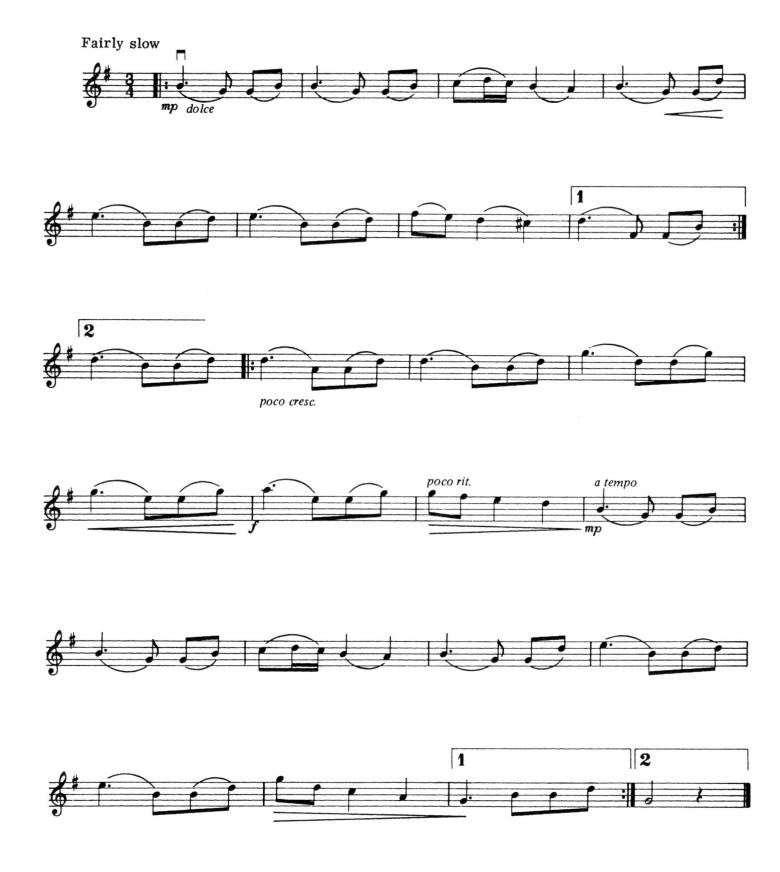

NORWEGIAN WOOD.

Words and Music by John Lennon and Paul McCartney.

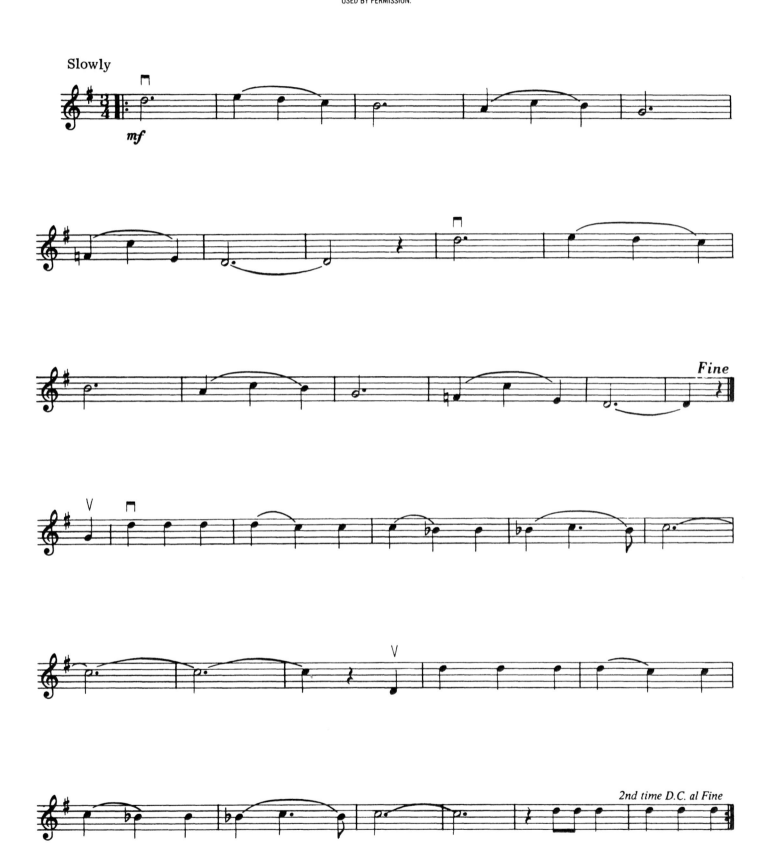

MOCKIN' BIRD HILL.

Words and Music by Vaughn Horton.

Bright waltz

SGT. PEPPER'S LONELY HEARTS CLUB BAND.

Words and Music by John Lennon and Paul McCartney.

Moderately bright

WOODEN HEART.

Words and Music by Fred Wise, Ben Weisman, Kay Twomey & Berthold Kaempfert.

Moderately (in 2)

HE'S GOT THE WHOLE WORLD IN HIS HANDS.

Traditional.

ARRIVEDERCI, ROMA.

Words by Renato Rascel. Music by Garinei & Giovanni. English lyric by Carl Sigman.

SEA OF HEARTBREAK.

Words and Music by Hal David & Paul Hampton.

OH WHAT A BEAUTIFUL MORNING.

Words by Oscar Hammerstein II. Music by Richard Rodgers.

RIVERS OF BABYLON.

Words and Music adapted by Bret Dowe and Trevor McNaughton.

SOME ENCHANTED EVENING.

Words by Oscar Hammerstein II. Music by Richard Rodgers.

DANNY BOY (LONDONDERRY AIR).

Traditional.

I DON'T KNOW HOW TO LOVE HIM.

Words by Tim Rice. Music by Andrew Lloyd Webber.

Moderato

THE FOOL ON THE HILL.

Words and Music by John Lennon and Paul McCartney.

WHEN I'M SIXTY-FOUR.

Words and Music by John Lennon and Paul McCartney.

LILLYWHITE.

Words and Music by Cat Stevens.

Moderato

RETURN TO SENDER.

Words and Music by Otis Blackwell and Scott Winfield.

Moderato

THE HAWAIIAN WEDDING SONG.

English Words by Al Hoffman and Dick Manning. Hawaiian Words and Music by Charles E. King.

Slowly

IMAGINE.

Words and Music by John Lennon.

Moderato

CONSIDER YOURSELF (FROM THE COLUMBIA PICTURES-ROMULUS FILM "OLIVER").

Words and Music by Lionel Bart.

FIDDLER ON THE ROOF.

Words by Sheldon Harnick. Music by Jerry Bock.

WITH A LITTLE HELP FROM MY FRIENDS.
Words and Music by John Lennon and Paul McCartney.

STRAWBERRY FIELDS FOREVER.

Words and Music by John Lennon and Paul McCartney.

REVIEWING THE SITUATION (FROM THE COLUMBIA PICTURES-ROMULUS FILM "OLIVER").

Words and Music by Lionel Bart.

Moderato

SHE LOVES YOU.

Words and Music by John Lennon and Paul McCartney.

Moderately, with a beat

LADY.
Words and Music by Lionel Ritchie, Jr.

PENNY LANE.
Words and Music by John Lennon and Paul McCartney.

WHO WILL BUY (FROM THE COLUMBIA PICTURES-ROMULUS FILM "OLIVER").

Words and Music by Lionel Bart.

ENGLISH DANCE.

J.C. Bach.

SURREY WITH THE FRINGE ON TOP.

Words by Oscar Hammerstein II. Music by Richard Rodgers.

Brightly

YOU NEVER DONE IT LIKE THAT.

Words & Music by Neil Sedaka & Howard Greenfield.

THEME FROM ROMEO AND JULIET.

Tchaikovsky.

KNOWING ME KNOWING YOU.

Words and Music by Benny Andersson, Stig Anderson and Bjorn Ulvaeus.

LA CUCARACHA.

Traditional.

THANK YOU FOR THE MUSIC.

Words and Music by Benny Andersson and Bjorn Ulvaeus.

HASTA MANANA.

Words and Music by Benny Andersson, Bjorn Ulvaeus and Stig Anderson.

JEALOUSY.

Words by Winfred May. Music by Jacob Gade.

POPCORN.
Music by Gershon Kingsley.

Moderato

MEXICAN HAT DANCE.

Traditional.

WHO DO YOU THINK YOU'RE KIDDING, MR. HITLER?

Words by Jimmy Perry. Music by Jimmy Perry and Derek Taverner.

AS LONG AS HE NEEDS ME (FROM THE COLUMBIA PICTURES-ROMULUS FILM "OLIVER").

Words and Music by Lionel Bart.

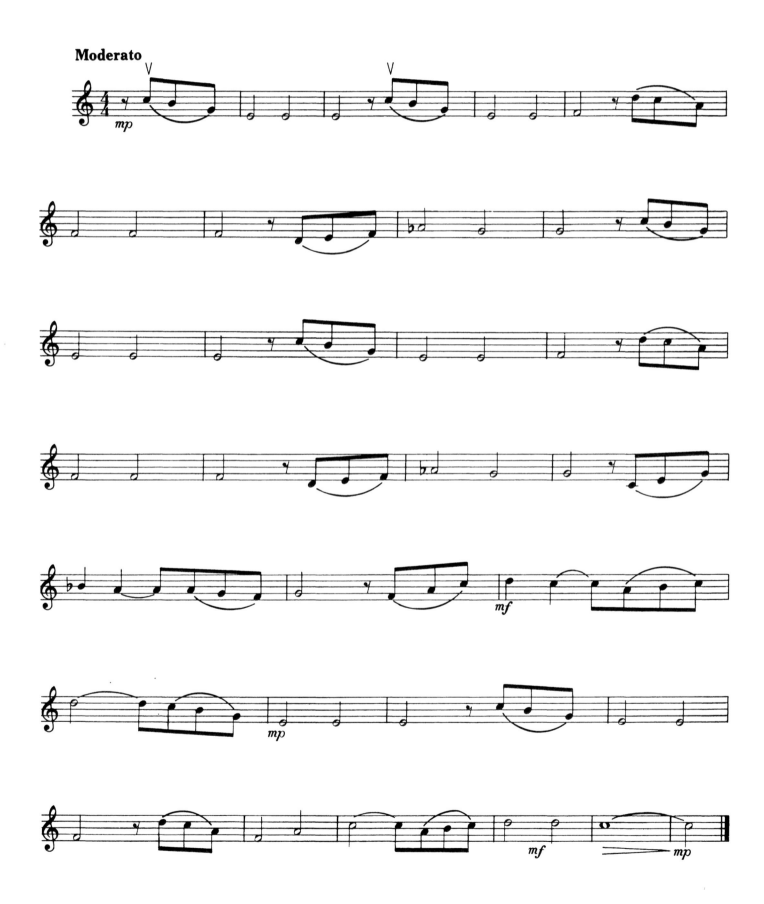

ANDANTE FROM FIFTH SYMPHONY.

Peter Tchaikovsky.

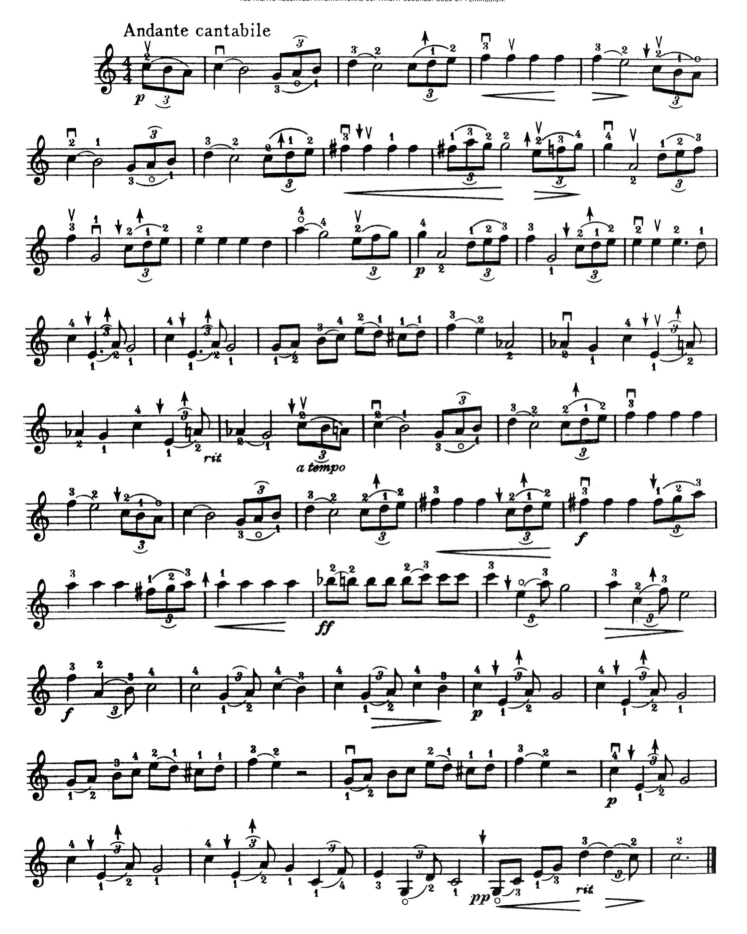

BARCAROLLE.

J. Offenbach.

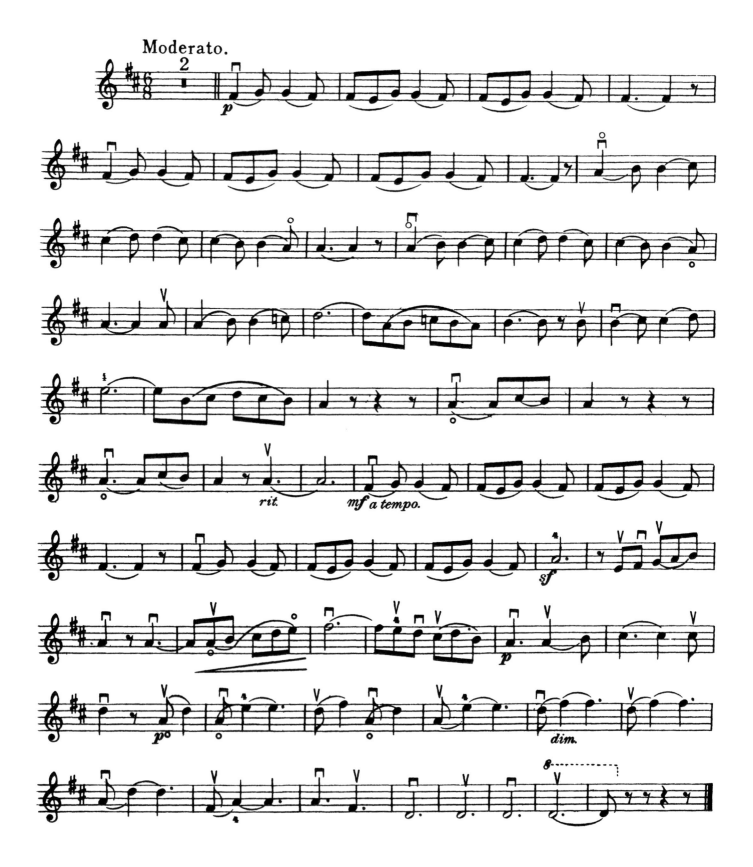

BEAUTIFUL DREAMER.

Stephen C. Foster.

BLUE DANUBE.

Johann Strauss.

THE BOATMEN'S SONG OF THE VOLGA.

Traditional.

(a) If desired the open A may be used in place of the 4th finger on the 3rd string

(b) If desired the open E may be used in place of the 4th finger on the 2nd string

CARNIVAL OF VENICE.

N. Paganini.

CELESTE AIDA.

G. Verdi.

a *If desired open A may be used in place of the 4th finger on the 3rd string*
b *If desired open E may be used in place of the 4th finger on the 2nd string*

CIELITO LINDO (BEAUTIFUL HEAVEN)

C. Fernandez.

COME BACK TO SORRENTO.

Ernesto de Curtis.

Allegretto - moderato
(Piano)

EMPEROR WALTZ.

Johann Strauss.

✿ In the first 16 bars the eighth notes may be played as quarter notes until bowing has become easy.

THE HAPPY FARMER.

Robert Schumann.

HUMOURESQUE.

Anton Dvorak.

Poco Lento e grazioso.
(*Rather Slow and graceful*)

INTERMEZZO.

Pietro Mascagni.

(a) If desired open A may be used in place of 4th finger on third string.
(b) If desired open E may be used in place of 4th finger on second string.
(c) Small F is optional.

LA PALOMA.

Sebastian Yradier.

LARGO FROM NEW WORLD SYMPHONY.

Anton Dvorak.

LIEBESTRAUM.

Franz Liszt.

Andantino

LOVE'S OLD SWEET SONG.

J.L. Molloy.

DRINK TO ME ONLY WITH THINE EYES.

Traditional.

MINUET IN G.

Beethoven.

NARCISSUS.

Ethelbert Nevin.

Moderate tempo
(Piano)

SABER DANCE.

Khachaturian.

SERENADE.

Franz Schubert.

(A) 4th finger stretched and touched lightly
(B) double notes ad libitum

THEME FROM CONCERTO NO. 1.

Tchaikovsky.

NOTE: The F natural on the E string appears often in this piece and particular attention should be paid to the playing of it.

THEME FROM CONCERTO NO. 2.

Rachmaninoff.

UNFINISHED SYMPHONY.

Franz Schubert.

Slowly with expression

WILLIAM TELL OVERTURE.

G. Rossini.

(a) If desired open A may be used in place of 4th finger on the 3rd string.

(b) If desired open E may be used in place of 4th finger on the 2nd string.

STEPTOE AND SON.

Music by Ron Grainer.

Moderato